Text and Illustrations Copyright © 2017 by Tymika Payne.
Address all inquiries to:
Email: icandoitseries@gmail.com

ISBN-13:
978-1947045064 (Baobab Publishing)

ISBN-10:
1947045067

AUTHOR BIOGRAPHY

Tymika Payne earned her Bachelors of Music Education degree and her Master's in Education Administration degree from Butler University. She has been an educator for over 22 years and has served children in elementary, middle, and high school levels. She and her husband currently reside in Indianapolis, Indiana with their 5 children.

DEDICATION

I would like to dedicate this book to my awesome husband Jefri Payne, my five AMAZING children Kentrell, Taylor, Jordyn, Danielle, and Paige, my supportive bestie LaVonne Jarrett, first lady Dwanda Washington, my wonderful mentors Tracy Palmer and Terry Dove-Pittman, my hilariously funny sister Marquita Robinson, and the inspiration that prompted me to write the book in the first place, my beautiful niece Madison Robinson. Love you and THANK YOU!

Rise and shine, it is morning time!
Myesha is ready to start her day.

"Good morning Myesha," her mommy said in a gentle voice. "Good morning Mama!" Myesha shouted.

"Mama! Mama! I have to go potty! I have to go NOW!" said Myesha. "Okay, let me help you out," her mother said.

Myesha's mother always helped her use the bathroom. But today Myesha was going to go potty without her mommy. "No, Mama! I can do it by myself!" Myesha shouted in an exciting voice.

"Ok Myesha," her mother said with a smile. "Go use the potty. I'm here if you need me."

"Ok Mama," Myesha said. She walked into the bathroom. She sat on her potty and waited, and she waited some more until finally…

14

She used the potty all by herself! "Mama, I did it! I used the potty by myself!" Myesha shouted.

"Yes, you're a big girl! You did it all by yourself."

"Wash your hands," her mother said. Myesha washed her hands and walked to the kitchen.

Myesha's mother looked at her with pride. "You are doing a GREAT job going to the potty by yourself! I am so proud of you!"

22

Myesha used the potty by herself again on Sunday, Monday, Tuesday, and even Wednesday.

She wanted to use the potty by herself...and she did just that!

The End!

Tymika's Tips for Potty Training

1. Teach your child how to communicate when they have to go! Use code words and/or hand signals to let you know that they have to use the pot.

2. Thirty minutes after drinking liquids, have them sit on the pot. Let your child have their favorite book or toy during this experience. This will help them relax and pass the time away while waiting for "magic" to happen!

3. After several successful experiences using the pot, begin to transition from diapers to pull-ups, and from pull-ups to underwear. Be patient...accidents may happen. However, your little one will get the hang of it.

4. Do not offer your little one anything to drink prior to bedtime. They should not have any type of beverage at least 1 hour prior to bedtime.

5. Make potty training FUN! Celebrate with them when they make it to the pot! Make it a BIG deal...sing, dance, and shout! Encouragement goes a long way!

32318327R00018

Made in the USA
Middletown, DE
04 January 2019